The Ink That Bleeds

Composed by:
Anthony Azzarito

Printed in the United States of America

First Printing: 2021
Updated Reprint: 2023
Published by: Vault Publishing
EST 2020
San Diego, CA

Reprint Published By: Poets Underground Press LLC

Composed & Written by Anthony Azzarito
Paperback ISBN: **978-1-5136-8087-3**

For my five children
For my dearest Sunny
For my family and friends
For my Poets Underground community
For my brothers in arms
For those who are disregarded
For the voiceless
> the unwanted
> the faithful
> the outcasts
> > and the diehards.

*"For I am the LORD your God who takes hold of your
right hand and **says** to you, **Do** not fear; I **will** help
you."*
Isaiah 41:13

Contents

SECTION TWO
THE DARKNESS THAT CONSUMED

Foreword

AN ERA OF CHANGE

Do you hear that?
It sounds like someone needs some help Certain individuals of the same race,
Thinking that they are a part of something.
But at the same time, they are falling down, divided. Which race, you might ask?
The human race.

So, stop, just pause for a second...
Open up your eyes and really take a gander... Don't walk away, ignoring your gut feeling Embrace your instincts...

America is bleeding and sobbing, crying loud as the television drowns her out. The red and blue are fading into the stripes of white
We are not united.
And it does matter about the crime, because our sin-tainted souls don't have a face, doomed since birth.
In my sick and twisted mind: extreme courses of action stem from core beliefs and if you believe in something or someone, you are accepting it as truth.
Having trust in it

Or having faith in that particular thing or hold a
strong opinion that someone is capable of
completing said action.
And I believe...

That we as flesh and blood and bones,
Homegrown
born on this earth, living mammals have the power
to make extreme courses of action, possible and
we have the power to change Whatever we want.
Why not?
Our founding for fathers created this nation and
they, themselves wrote laws based on what was
suitable for their life- style and challenges they
faced during that era,
what they believed in...
So, I mean,
Why are people so quick to believe that we CAN
NOT
cure racism,
stop war across the seas
provide food shelter and electricity to all 3rd world
countries
Promote love in all forms
Or have real, absolute change in this great nation...
No, of course not, but...

You want to trust actors in movies, entrepreneurs,
political figures, and other celebrities; only by what
you see and hear on T.V. because they are famous,

You believe in your asshole boss whom you hate, the one you pretend to be cool with, so you don't get fired or left out at the company Christmas parties
You trust in your parents even though they have physically and verbally abused you. You trust in our voting system and election process
You believe what the game show host with the great hair and sexy body has to say because you fancy a good time with her in your dreams
You believe the car salesman when he says he'll get you a big discount when you are looking at a brand-new car to buy
You trust in our freedom, the American Dream, the 27 amendments, you trust in the laws that are meant to protect us while they are being constantly broken each and every single day.
You believe in a justice system that has proven to be un-just in so many ways
You believe the weatherman, lead anchors, and sports cast announcers on the channel 6 news You trust in archaeologists, historians, mechanics, teachers, professors,
even the popular chicks in high school and of course you believe in the President, right? Some believe that the earth is flat, and that space does not exist.

You place your trust in science
You believe God is not real even when it says In God We Trust on the back of US currency,

You believe God is not real when his name is in our pledge of allegiance
You believe God is not real even when there are periodic time date names referenced as "A.D." or "B.C." That stands for Anno domini (in the year of our Lord) and before Christ
You trust what your grandfather says about the military now because he was in Vietnam
You believe what is said in newspapers, textbooks, magazines, IG posts, memes, YouTube videos,

website articles, gossip columns, and even nutrition facts labels
You believe that it's a good idea to buy a lottery ticket You believe in winning at casinos
You trust your family even if they lie, steal, or cheat
You trust credit card companies, bank tellers and accountants, yoga instructors, maybe even waiters and cashiers
You trust your drug dealers and the DMV
You believe in that the random rich old white guy; the one with his name on perfect picket signs- shoved
in the grass in front of houses and businesses, the one who you have never met or seen in person in your town, saying how he will actually make a difference in YOUR community, only if you vote for him for city council or mayor.
You trust in cops, firefighters, state officials, lawyers, judges, doctors, postal workers, delivery

personnel, taxi drivers, tax consultants, realtors,
investment advisers, and the sweet old lady that
lives
next door because she bakes a pie for you on your
birthday.
Anyone would believe what these people say even
if it was the first time you ever met them. Call it a
figment of human nature.
You trust in certain foods being "all natural,"
"fresh from the farm," having no GMOs, or
"organic" because it's stated by an official sticker
slapped on there by the USDA.

You trust in dating websites
You believe in capital punishments and 2nd
chances
You believe in good and evil, right and wrong, fate,
karma, Ying and Yang or even Zen.
You trust your zodiac sign readings and what they
represent based off astrology

Some believed that the world was going to end in
2012
You trust in the power of free will

And some believe in the butterfly effect

You trust in holy matrimony but don't believe in
divorce

You believe that women aren't allowed to have
abortions while men aren't even held accountable
for abandoning their children
You trust in dietary plans, weight loss pills, and
chemically produced supplements You believe in
the pursuit of happiness
You trust in the US government, FBI, CIA, ATF, CDC
and NSA
There are some who believe in the Illuminati, the
NWO, and the Freemasons
You believe in life and death
Some only trust themselves but hate all other
people, while some hate themselves but trust all
other people
You trust in the means of equality
You believe that taking your own life will fix all of
your problems
You trust in technology, machines, and artificial
intelligence

You trust in the public-school systems
You believe in musicians, artists, visionaries, public
speakers, reverends,
mathematicians, CEOs,
inventors, and world class athletes
So why not believe in me?

I'll tell you why because there is a fine line between
wants and needs
Payments and good deeds

Along with solid forward progression, actual proof
of success- instead of just a great thought, idea or
proclamation.
Well, I am here to truly move people forward.
With no fear, and nothing to stop me, or silence
me,
I know some of those nouns are blindly trusted,
easy to trust, hard to believe, trusted by default,
mandatory to believe in, or some have legitimate
reasons or credentials that developed people to
trust or believe in.
So put me on that list of things you believe in or
trust
You need to believe in change.
Because I believe in change.
I am just a poet,
One who hopes people will believe in;
to change the world.

Section One
The Unwavering Light

LET THE INK BLEED

Let the ink bleed, let it seep through the pages
Feel the emotions underneath all of the unwanted
wages Nothing is free.
          happiness comes with a price to pay just like
everything else
The men made into heroes; they are the ones who
store greed on a dusty shelf

A pun upon my words can sometimes be very vague
But the lesson behind my thoughts can be very harsh
to fake

Call it larceny, I take what I want and leave my soul
in ruins
But isn't that how great poets struck up a storm and
started movements? Inspiring humans not to be just
humans
Pick apart the rhymes and dissect my mind
Break my bones and misinterpret the tone
When there is nothing left to see, when everything
has been kept out of reach
An idea will still remain.

You cannot kill an idea, it is as tough as metal chains
Solid like stone graves, an idea has a chance to make
a change
That chance can be lost in an instant

A shot that could have been made but you missed it

Now listen, put your ear to the wall and hear an ill-
tempered scream
One that could transfer dreams into the plot or
theme
A cry that makes the hair stand up on your sleeves
I've heard this sound, it's like a constant ringing in
my ears
I'll still listen because it blocks out my frightful fears

It is fear that drives me
It is God who guides me
And it is pain that resides in me
Yet I still stand tall and keep that idea close to me
This idea is a secret that not even the police could
breach
Branches on a tree that are tools used to teach
But all it needs is for someone to plant a seed
Someone to see, what it means to just...
Let the Ink Bleed.

SCORPIO

I started as a rebel who needed an escape
Took life for granted, and lost control of my fate
A misplaced puddle of toxic waste
In an ocean full of plastic and chunks of shark
bait
Can be affected-by demons that delegate
I'm going to demonstrate
Exactly how to increase the knowledge base
My therapist, is an inanimate object
Pen marks clog her perspective on certain topics
She's my sponsor and my conscious
Concealed conversations, exposing skeletons in
my closets
I'm pushing thirty now, and I still have dreams
Objects in the mirror are getting closer than
they seem
For instance, I now have aching pains in my
knees
I used to run for miles in the sand on the beach
We can't hide the matches and then ask for
cheap gasoline
No wonder we struggle with daily routines
It's not just us parents it's also the teens
So, take a moment and accept your hand
Every card could be bent but it's worth the
chance
It's a complicated story that only some will
understand

You label me like a blank poster
Thinking out loud, I have to stay sober
Transform chaos into culture
As your soul always becomes much colder

But never lose site-of what matters most
My life's written in riddles
With rapid lines, of simple civil jokes
Scoop out my eyes but leave air in my throat
Audacious; now that's a bold adjective
I wear a disguise but have no magic tricks
No fashion, no props, and no happiness
So, use me as the learning curve
Because I got bridges to burn and passion to
purge
Pain and misery were none of my concern
This world will always be ripped apart
Born sinners till the end, dead poets from the
start

THE HERO

Capes, costumes, superpowers
Corny one liners by a good-looking cast,
A dainty damsel in distress
      Yeah, this isn't that type of comic book
      superhero story.
Fade in.

Here to date is an average white male that has
defeated the gruesome trials of substance
dependency
Finding his place in a divided society
Along with balancing a good relationship with
his wife for the last 10 years
AND being a father to 3 young boys.
...to some people those actions are
mundane,
ordinary,
easy.

    (I will literally drop whatever I'm doing and,
      with a cold beer and a crooked smile,
        love to hear what anyone has to say
      about how easy it is to raise children.)

The moment when little babies are able to fly in
a newly painted purple sky with talking animals
after money grows on trees...
Is when and only then is when that will be
accurate.

So, our non-caped, long board cruising, vans
wearing, rap and hip hop lovin,' main character
is a broken
nail in a haystack.
One of a kind.
        Spends his days looking out into the
public, on the T.V., on social media apps,
while carefully listening to music for any hint of
crime to battle with his pen.
        That is his weapon
What makes him the hero of this story is his
ability to write.

The power of ink can be metamorphic
His code he lives by is simple,
        we fight with the words we write
Throw that on a giant spotlight up in the
atmosphere for the city to stare at
                Wouldn't that be nice.

The greatest attack on a world full of villains,
killers, politics, terrorists, and even masked men
Is writing.
        Literature.
                Something to read.
Throughout history; history has been written.
All of our past mistakes, victories, downfalls,
and new discoveries have been documented
Hands have been put to work.
Those blistering, car-pool tunneled, cramping
hands
Heroes do not only live in movies or fairytales
They are born as regular people choosing to
attempt the impossible and achieve
extraordinary outcomes in sometimes difficult
situations.

Those are heroes.
That is what I hope to accomplish.
I hope that my words and sentences can
somehow cure racism, save people from suicide,

be a self-help
guidebook for battling inner demons.

I think I can be a hero.

But that's only based off what you think a hero
is defined as,
The audience, the viewers, readers and
visionaries alike
        Well, I think I hear an angered teen
shouting up to the heavens.
                Time to suit up and leave it all on the page
                Goodbye for now.
Fade out.

THE I.D.E.A.

There's always been a whisper inside my heart,
like a distant echo through an abandoned town,
telling me... "anyone has the ability to change
the world."

That idea as a whole is one of the dearest things
imbedded in my soul,
It's an idea that only one could feel when it's
raining outside
When you have a cozy cup of crisp coffee in
your hand
And stare off into the distance and then begin to
wonder,
What is the true power of an idea...?

Does one man have one chance to change
millions of minds a million times?
Do ideas ever go farther if the missed
opportunities don't catch the light?
Are they forgotten, waiting to be recycled by
another being...?

The mind of a poet works in various ways,

One can either project his pain upon the pages
in pursuit of passion
or there's another way, where it's just a hobby
that helps the days go by a sliver of a second
slower.

When I put thoughts on paper, I save opinions
for later and just let my brain savor...
The ability to write...
The moment...

The freedom.
The feeling of
that no matter what happens in this life, the
moment you're reading the context of someone's
mind,

You are consumed with so many different
emotions, experiences, and events
It's euphoric.

I try to incorporate a common ground between
reader and writer when I let the ink bleed
There's an everlasting want and need for a poet
to have someone else connect the dots,
...to read between the lines,
...to see the cracks in the cement,
...to have that lightbulb turn on inside.

So, my idea starts with words taking the form of
pillars to hold up the beliefs of the voiceless,
It goes on making a time of day where people
are taught to look for human connection
through music and poems,
...rather than appearances and status quo.

Creativity and character are more important
than the money you have or your sexual stature.

I mean, What about your dreams?
What about that constant scratching at the skull
of a sickening IDEA...?
Imagine, develop, evolve and acknowledge.

That is where I leave you, with some room to
establish, to expand...to embellish.

An idea is potent
An idea can start a revolution
An idea can stop a century of chaos
An idea is the content of your cognition
An idea can save a relationship that once was
broken of words not said
An idea to me is simple, it's priceless, and it's
bold.
What does an idea mean to you?
What ideas can you create based off my clues?

A POET'S AMBITION

I feel alone when I'm surrounded by minds that
aren't free
Wasting their lives away with insignificant ideas,
portraits, or suggestions of how to "live life"
You have no business in telling others the
meaning of something that you, YOURSELF, are
still searching for.
The fact is- it will always remain unknown.
The big question...what is our purpose for?

Songs are secrets within words, and words speak
to me the way other humans and creatures of
that sort...really never have.
I mean why does there need to be a "meaning" to
life...aren't we all here just to,
EXIST.

Blue skies turn black, when you've lost that voice
inside you that screams, continue pushing
forward!
But most people don't, they are depressed,
defeated, distant...

For me, I struggle with time; that's one beast, at
the very least, has shown everyone that it
CHEATS
I've always dwelled in the darkness, but my soul
is still shining bright,

so, shout out loud from the deepest part of your
heart.

Empty out all that empathy... in your left cargo
pocket that you've been carrying around,

all that lint, all that dust, everything that is
meaningless. I hope now you will feel free.

Let me tell you of an image in my mind, that life
offers-it involves things most find ominous and
a bit strange,
Like walking through a deserted wasteland with
graffiti on the walls,
imagining what memories were made here while
the sun sets,
venturing off to places that have clear, concise
examples of where time has shown us...that it is
real.
We all know there's times where we wish it
didn't
plus, colors always seem brighter after we've
indulged in some adrenaline.

If I could have a plate of that with a glass of
bliss on the rocks, that would be nice!
We all have that fabricated fantasy of what life is
supposed to be,
based off what's on T.V., honestly stop blinking
and just live.

Because somewhere- A father fears for his
family that might forget his figure,
if he so happens to die in the midst of fighting
for a much bigger picture.

DO YOU UNDERSTAND WHAT I'M SAYING?
The problems that you deal with every single
day, aren't weighed on a different scale,
they aren't considered to be some type of Holy
Grail,
while some other man's credit card debt is seen
as an empty old pale?

Bartering isn't an option, there's no top bidder
here, this piece of meat will never end up on the
chopping block,
Sorry LUCY, and you won't get my soul. You
have to believe it, when you say it, you know?

So, feel the cool breeze, kiss the side of your
cheek as you and your loved one ride through
the city,
engage in a game with a companion that still
shares the same vision.

There's complete and utter freedom in the act of
scrutiny,
asking officials what we are really free from, but
most will only mutter, mutiny.
But that is why I do it
I say it's our GOD given right to question,
why settle for less of something that the
president failed to mention,
That is why I keep my pen filled with ink
That is why this gift is something no man *can*
take from me

That is why the greatest characteristic a
visionary has is the ability to think
That is why I simply love to dream.
Let's make these words and phrases, the
meaning to which others think their life should
be.
Everyone will still do it...
But I believe in change, I'm here to dissect the
same emotions that other's might have inside
their brain

I can put it on paper for you,
I can make it...something you can touch,
something you can feel,
It's last burning ember in a dying fire, will it be
concealed?

TIME

As time becomes clockwork and nothing more
Silence is something never again to ignore
Everlasting within minds
Spent eighteen years down a self-paved path
Searching for solitude to confine inner wrath
Recognition has just resigned

Unknowingly thinking of all mistakes, I have made
Time ticks a sliver of a second slower
Because God never showed me how to pray
Delayed with disbelief in clocks controlling our lives
I question the reason behind freedom
Without some sense of motion no one survives

In due time we will understand the unknown
Living life long and limitless
Until we accept the pit as our home

Bestowing in non-baptized belief
Time will only tell
If there's rhyme within relief

TURN THE PAGE

God gives gifts, willingly,
I write these rhymes quite viscously
Some might say it's calligraphy,
It comes from my free minded will to think,
Please pick apart my beliefs,
Written in chalk on the concrete,
Never too rotten to stuff your cheeks,
So come on and have a blast with me,
With your mascots in your dreams
And then you won't be haunted by the words you
failed to speak,
Like a pastor trying to preach to kids that smoke
weed and drink,
This outlet is much more than what you see,
On any channel on T.V. Or magazine.
So, we zone into the present, the stage is set,
Turn on the radio to hear a waste of breath,
Amateurs act as artists claiming zero intellect
Giving rap a bad rep

Producing weak punchlines that refer back to sex,
And the way they dress,
It probably came from Marilyn Manson's personal
desk.
And even if the devil himself said that I'd be next,
Man, I wouldn't sign any of his damn paychecks.

It's only about getting people to say YES!
Living this life with No Regrets!
Starring into the eyes of death
Corduroy Suite, I'll look my best

Front page news, with rhymes so fresh
Precious time has now been spent,
True talent remains to be dormant,
 I've been sitting so long up in the bullpen that
there's dirt clogging up in my storm vent,
I'm here to spit real life emotions and prepare a
feast,
There's food for thought here as my words act as
therapy,
To help the public and diseased see my rhymes as
remedies,
So, when every addict or fiend,
Chump, bully, or average teen-feels alone and
needs to scream,
My voice can be the Golden Fleece,
To shield them from the need to make themselves
bleed,
Becoming absolutely free from any chains that
suffocate their inner peace,
This shit is much bigger than just me, so just
breathe.
.

THE LEAVES

Take note of what you see
does it match what you need?
Look at the cracks within the concrete
Or reasons behind every step below your feet.

Maybe the wind can act as your relief
brushing away every unwanted thought of your
dreams

Then there's the leaves
Only living if they're one with the trees
Examples of peace

No matter the color they are, they all came from
seeds
All together floating down onto the streets
Never giving into the world's deceit
Everyone else only plays for keeps

Especially the demons that make you disagree
I stray away from those trees
Charred bark peeling

A lesson earned when you become free

So, trust in the meanings behind the ink
And anything from ancient beliefs

I want you to take note of what you see
Maybe then you'll appreciate
the simplicity of the leaves

AUDIO TACTICS

I place my ear to the ground
feeling bits of grainy sand all over the coarse
cement, on my cheek
desperately awaiting.
for something unheard of, to speak

A faint cry for help from a distant land
screams of an abled body willing to make a
change
or maybe it appears in the songs of yesterday

I do not know what I am listening for, but I'll
know what it is, when I hear it.

I begin to analyze, develop, and evolve;
And I will seize the appropriate moment
when it arrives.

Then I shall respond in a manner that needs no
explanation
I am one who puts emotions into strokes of ink;
for that alone is a power some do not possess.
My existence in reality is consumed with what
my ears can hear
If I had to, I'd choose audio over visual on any
day of the week.

So, the air is crisp, the moon is bright
The traffic is loud and obnoxious

An owl begins his nightly tune
And the crowds are nothing short of alive

Here, there are so many different octaves of
noise; my thoughts scatter, but my pen is
mightier than
Distraction.
None of these distractions is the clamor of the
voiceless
No alarm to ignite a revolution.

So, I will keep on listening
for the sound.
I will continue on; keeping my ear to the ground.

TEENAGE YEARS

There was a time where there was nothing on
my mind,
Except the number of friends, I had and who I
would find.
Those are missed memories that I want back,
We all need a sense of happiness and joy that I
lack.
In this world we should never have regrets,
because all that I have done, I will never forget.
Photographs of all my loved ones,
With possessions left from all night, non-stop
fun.

Summer days are here and back again,
Late nights at the movies, to hanging out with
my friends.
Teenage years always getting the best of me,
Now I remember the good life oh so vividly.

There is always room for harsh mistakes,
We are the type of people who think nothing is
fake.
We live our lives with heart in hand,
An all or nothing attitude is what we demand.
We are the ones that don't get knocked down,
We are the ones that have never seen a frown.
The amount of adrenaline that we consume,
Will keep us going until we've reached our
doom.

Summer days are here and back again,
Late nights at the movies, to hanging out with
my friends.

Teenage years always getting the best of me,
Now I remember the good life oh so vividly.

We only have so much time to live,
Don't worry about the lists, just remember what
you did.
Never stop loving the people that returned the
favor,
Seeing the sun set, is where we all become
braver.
This is where my memories have been made,
This is what some friends have saved,
This is how much my life means to me,
This is why I write for everyone to see.

A MAN'S BURDEN

As men we have a certain way of living
that we unknowingly embraced
Let me tell you
there is a payment of suffering, when you enroll
into manhood
A moment in time where the boy can no longer
be a boy
so, the man appears
the man deep within his consciousness
Reality hits like pounds of bricks
the young soul is tattered by fear
tangled in a web of lies.
Soon I needed to drink, so I consumed more
than my share
I bummed a drag, I became an addict
I wanted to feel love, so I chiseled at multiple
hearts
I longed to become free, so the mirrors I
shattered gave me a lifetime of bad luck
And with that bad luck, I became dangerous.
You see, we only have proof that life exists if we
accept what we hear, taste, smell...and especially
what
we can touch and see.

As humans, we are taught to find a purpose or a
meaning to life
But what if the meaning to life ceases to exist?
Then do we lose all hope?

When does the chaos come full circle to become
tolerable?
As a man, I was taught that there is no progress
without struggle

Work hard and expect nothing in return
You are only as good as your last fuck up.
No, I will break that cycle.
I'm supposed to show others, examples of what
life is like, from a human being point of view
Human beings being humans.
even then the seeds we plant now, we have to
make sure they grow into trees
I must leave steppingstones for my children's,
children
when their path, gets too blurry to see,
I provide that last name that they will carry
forward
That is my job as a man, as a Father.

Someone once told me, damaged goods never
sell at full price
I took that in the aspect of our souls.
You won't get 100% of what you bargained for.
your present happiness will not be greater than
your eternal pain.
You will lose the most precious thing you own
and the salesman will just laugh and tally
another one his earnings.

There'll be no mercy
No second chances
No extra lives.

So, when the time comes and you need to stand
up and be a man,

Remember that day
Remember what I've said
Remember the place where you no longer lived
as one of the boys
Remember the true burden of being a Man.

OUT THE WINDOW

I stare out my bedroom window
With frivolous wonder.
Wishing; that one day,
the wide-open plains, salty blue oceans,
greasy highways, flashy city blocks
and the smoggy atmosphere
Will welcome me into their habitats.
A vast graveyard of endless opportunities;
Blood-soaked soil,
Or a false reality?
You choose.
This place: it's just a bad soap opera that ends
with the entire cast dying and somehow the
narrator is the father, who planned it all.
My imagination has always got the best of me
But it has always existed.
I might not achieve my dreams, but I still dream
and have hope
And courage.
I ponder on the thought of living in a world
where humans don't place their trust in
machines
more so than their own race.
Maybe it's the era we grew up in or just a flaw to
being imperfect,
A drastic change or a so-called evolution might
serve us well.
Because without passion all phenomena are
puny, insignificant.
Without inner peace, the love of oneself; man
cannot love others, lead others.
It starts there.

I stare out a crusty, under-maintained window of
a white school bus
that's at full capacity.
No phones, no food, no radio
Thinking to myself, in a strange voice inside my
own head, "What did I get myself into?"
As other men are staring at their own reflections
thinking the same.
We are but humbled souls
thrown into the lion's den
Almost instantaneously, regret comes taping
violently at my door.
Reminding me that even my conscious isn't
satisfied with my decisions,
But I can't go back.
An easy path isn't jagged and complex, it's
smooth and laid out before you,
No need for the struggle.
Nonetheless,
I notice that there are no lap belts as I plop my
meat suit down upon a tattered brown seat,
only silence and fear are present here
The calm before the storm.
Doors open.
The cussing and pushing
and shoving and screaming
and shouting and barking of orders swiftly begin
just as tornados tragically tear through towns.
My bones rattle
My skin is itchy and wet
My heart beats out of my chest

The debt to be paid for a pair of boots and
camouflage.

Two different views of life through
two different peep holes
I comprehend far beyond what my eyes allow me
to see
Way past the horizon.
A window is simply there acting as a barrier just
in case; whatever you are gazing at, a glimpse of
it, is all that you get.
You must become the part of the picture to
prove the point
In order to be seen
Or exist out in the world
One must be truly awake
And alive.

LETTER TO THE PRESIDENT

I swear I know your past, but can you tell me my
future
Don't regret this life
It's the only true gift
On this great night, spread no lies
To those who need to listen
And be one with Him, Himself
Walking through minefields of careless mistakes
While walking through life not thinking of
careless mistakes
It's very unlikely for that to happen, life isn't
what it used to be
Change this world dramatically
We're due for a revolution
Could this be true, unraveling a clue?
To why the streets are black
still filled with hope
Walking through minefields of mistakes
While walking through life not thinking of my
careless mistakes
The middle class has a story to tell
Don't treat our lives as if we are in hell
Souls are the best way to invest, not for sale

WE ARE ANARCHY

World with laws and democracy
I say that isn't the life for me
Lands of corrupt passion for power
No one lives in peace
Everyone is afraid, poor or just plain cowards
A world without any government
Teens and fleas,
All roaming so free
Roads without names or meaning
Sounds like a perfect place
Sounds like my one dream

We are the rebels
Ones whose thoughts are extreme
We are the rebels
Where our homes are the streets
Never caring about the world of tomorrow
Never know where will eat
But we drown our enemies in sorrow
The government doesn't exist in our lands
Carrying guns and drugs
Some things will never again be up for demand
Because this is our anarchy
Where religion is still a legend
And I'm still here to defend it

Danger can be vast
No police or any type of enforcement
Horrific crime will happen all so fast
Nothing can beat this type of freedom
As the whole world implodes
Have my brothers and family living without
reason

We are merely a glimpse of the resistance
We don't break the law
Because it's staying out there in the distance
One thousand miles down the road
Are all the lost and weak souls
Underneath the rats and all the moles
Anarchy saved me from death
Couldn't live the American life
Defiance was always my first step

We are all lonely men
From a world full of lies, now and forever
The image of freedom will be in our eyes

WHY WAR?

You hear the bombs dropping
And their talks stopping
Never mind about the treasures under your bed
Keep your friends close, they might end up dead

War is upon us in so many ways
Everyone has a purpose
Time to say what you really need to say
Don't be afraid to question one's thoughts
Your life is what you make of it
Down with politicians and executive officers
People make this country what it is today
We always try to make crime pay
Freedom has its rights and flaws
Having to obey so many worthless laws
The government should be afraid of its people
Without them, country becomes so feeble
I live my life with heart in hand
So much to live for, so much demand
And we ask ourselves, why war?
I ask myself the same question,
But no one knows what we are fighting for

Everything has a purpose on this earth
Nobody knows what they're worth
But yet we still hate
Sometimes no reason, maybe just weight
There will never be peace
Somebody, somewhere, they will want more
So, I ask again, why war?

When our lives are consumed by death
Then maybe we will know who or what's left

But until then, I'm going to live the life of
freedom
And nothing is going to stop my dreams, not
even death
Think of war as a contract
And no one read the fine print

BATTLE CRY

Raise your fists in the air because we are alive,
you'll find a voice wrapped up in this surprise
Zero under ONE
Believe it or not we are one.
Our world isn't perfect -it has some cracks and
fault lines, but we as humans have learned how
to prevail.
Look at what we've accomplished, or if you can't
do that...be proud of what YOU yourself has
accomplished.
No matter who's the president, or the amount of
hatred for the opposite gender, race, religion,
color, ethnicity, sexual preference, or social
status...
we still are still here!
And if you are constantly shaking your head
from west to east and completely disagree with
what I'm trying to preach
You might think-that of all the racial profiling
and prejudice and extremist acts of "terror" that
is present in reality is scary and you feel afraid.
You feel defeated ...and you now become
stagnant
After you stay in a place for so long, you become
that place
Do not become what the enemy wants you to
become
No matter what, we as humans are obligated to
adapt and overcome any obstacle to achieve the
desired outcome at any cost!
And if you are not killer, it's time to kill those
negative counterproductive beliefs and
make a change

Because we will prosper
And I truly BELIEVE that.
I believe in the United States
I believe in humanity
I believe that a single act of love or kindness can
pull the darkest people out of the blackest
shadows
I believe the people have a voice
I believe in due diligence
I believe in an idea
And that idea is simple...
What if history can repeat itself and a man's
words could actually change life as we know it?
What if my sentences and phrases could cure
racism or even move mountains?
What if?
What if we started to fight and used this is our
Battle Cry.

RETURNING FROM THE DEAD

Life isn't always what it's cut out to be
Been thrown so many change ups and curves
Don't know what to throw away or what to keep
This life could have had a brighter side
Still think of all my mistakes
25 years and I'm still looking for somewhere to
hide

Just thinking of how to keep this body relaxed
For the amount of anger inside
Mind always has bad memories within
Now going to rewrite life's timeline
Show my family who this man is
Hang on everyone, I promise to pay back every
dime
Coming back from the dead can be an
impossible thing
But how my life is and what I'm trying to do
It's like I'm asking the devil to sing with me.

Nothing can run me off my path
There's always going to be things in my way
All I have to do is stop and just laugh
Life's too short to be pissed off all the time
Have to keep those voices out of head
Keep control of this mind, which is rightfully
mine

Thinking and trying all to hard
Friends and enemies place aside conflicts
Happiness isn't going to be that far
I'm not the only one trying to make the pieces fit
Someone out there feels the same

And someone's out there to tell him to quit

All I've ever wanted to do
Is wild, loose, and carefree
The dream that became reality
Is this now something I must fulfill?
Going to put my all into this life
No need to start this God-forsaken flight.

THIS IS WHO I AM

This is who I am
Death can't even stop me
Rebel against with just my hands
Go ahead and start to judge
Still hating in harmony
My life won't end in tragedy
Now using this pen as a knife to kill
These pages of ink will be the last thing you feel

Even in the cloudy night
Death is infatuated by fright
In the mirror is a deadly man
Whose wise words state
Who I truly am?
The one that does know how to kill
But doesn't know who to trust
What he sees or how to feel
Others hate on him with much despair
Non-baptized beliefs tell him not to care

As legendary light shines through
You will soon become amused
Fearing the sight of all my fate
I will never falter
Until the world is rid of all the hate
As the devil asks for a dance
I keep on writing without being worthy of wealth
A rebel yell stating not a chance
Deceit is deprived by gold
And now greed cannot be in my soul

NO COMPLY

People fish for cash donning a cursed mask
Old habits that led to an adverse past
Been accused of crimes,
I've had to free my mind,
 We're labeled as a basket case.
Thoughts fly away,
ink drops blot the page
Caught the dire straits
Roadblocks at higher rates
Clickbait, cyberspace,
Wires in flames
Stay quiet or hibernate,
I remain awake
Rapping for some change,
These fists are raised
Maybe some acid rain,
can erase this hate
Tattered flags wave,
so, rewind the tapes
No time to celebrate,
 Riots are underway
Protest, behave,
or dig your own graves
Dreadful weights
Placed on every race
Welcome all plagues,
because America's fake
From Cali to Spain,
we are stomping on snakes.

LYRICAL EXPANSION

I am an arrogant loser
Anger is apparently truant
Music creates movements
It's written in our genes
To educate the foolish
While producing new hits
Spilling wisdom like Confucius
To battle the disbelief
Matter of fact it's just a disguise
Pills only artists prescribe
Let the corruption die
So, the fat lady can sing
All the gangster jokes
Mixed with meaningless flows
Leads to a system overload
We need a fire hose,
with a new sales pitch
Damage is catastrophic
And I am the fail switch.
Icebergs in sight steering the Titanic
Crashing isn't part of my planning
There are lessons needed to be managed
As God commands it
I shall polish and I brand it
Brainstorming outstanding
Listen close for this
Lyrical expansion

RED ROSE

My darling you are the only one I love
Like a rose, you are the desire
You are the burning fire
That grows in me day by day

Your pedals are beautifully smooth
Your leaves are green with envy
Your touch is the one I sooth
I love the way you're different than all the others
You're just like me
I care for you like my blood brother

You were beautiful in the garden of love
It was a miracle from above
That I found you my baby
Like a rose, you bloom with the sunrise
Our relationship- it never dies

I love you baby,
Respect to you- I guarantee
Like a rose, you're luscious and tender
That one night we had
I will always and forever, remember

Your smell is as sweet as snow
I know there won't be any more pain
Like a rose in the rain
You're much more beautiful
If I die for you tonight
Lastly, I would want to see your gentle smile

My darling you are the only one I love, you are...
The only one that keeps my heart
The only one who makes me live
The only one I want by my side
The only one I would die for tonight.

I DON'T KNOW IF I LOVE YOU

When it's the end of life as we know it
I'll explain my feelings for you
And some things I have to admit
We define love as a tangible thing
People always saying the three words so much
Along with daytime walks during the spring

I say to you that I like you
Because love will make my life hell
You don't understand, you love me without a
clue
I want to say I truly am in love
The day dawns on me during this dim
to these lies that you speak of

Doing what is wrong is what I know
Right is always so hard to find
Along with increasing my status quo
I'm not saying hello, I'm not saying goodbye
I'm making sure this is the life I want
Because the art of lust has always caught my eye

I SHALL NOT SURRENDER

Drenched in sorrow from days of pain
This beautiful moon will be ours to claim
I promise my heart will soon be sewn
By now it's my feelings that you'll always own

Don't break the chain
Don't fade away
Never let go
Of this amazing grace

Keeping my mind steady, being true to my resist
By now I shall learn patience
Then know when to prepare the perfect kiss
So, into the Garden of Eden, I will pick
A special flower that will clearly show
My sins on the pedal just about to drip

Take this in my name
Take hold and grasp
For how each one is different
To tell us if love will last

As crazy as it sounds, I'm dead man
It's you who's made me hurt myself
And become someone that I can't stand
To escape these thoughts of depression
My knees can't break, my head has to rise
It's time to take me home with you
And flush away all of my demise

Walking blindly into the house of lust
Knowing I've been a frequent visitor with broken
trust

FOOLISH GAME

Walking through this Hell I just need a place to
rest,
Every demon that I see slides a thumb across his
neck
Telling me that my turn's coming up here on the
left
I'm about see some bodies who've completely
lost their heads,
They opened up the Gates and I was blinded by
the light,
I didn't know where I was going, I didn't think I
was alright,
Last night was the last time I had opened up my
eyes
And I still had a grasp a hold of my knife, what a
sight,
having too much pain and having too much
misery
Even in the midst of fame, fear was still with me
Such a mystery,
to why we become a part of the history,
 but certainly not the time
Developing harsh rhymes laced within my
rotten-lost mind,
It's about to cost me my damn life,
And at the same time,
 landmines lay where I have crossed over and
over again,
The motion of the cold shoulder grows colder
and colder again,

Friends become foes, they continue to loosen up
their split ends,
Be my guest and pop your top of your own
compulsive heads,
Everyone is so repulsed and starts to boast
about their freedom,
But please tell me what are we really free from?
Is this the ending of a story that the devil reads
from?
I'm locked inside a prison with open doors and
empty hallways
Demons keep slipping through, they're
hollowing out the crawl space,
Itching and scratching at something like a false
face,
And I'm just hoping Saint Peter will actually let
me in
For playing a game that Should have never had
the chance to begin

So, tell me what you want, I'm running off this
path,
Don't try to take my pride, all I'll do is laugh,
I'm a little broken down but that's just from my
past,
I'm never going to sign the dotted line; I see the
facts.
The only dancing I'm doing, is going to be with
my wife
Don't act like there's no one down here trying to
collect my life
Are you trying to say that no one ever has
thought like me?
While you're hiding in the shadows, disguised in
deceit,

Whispering your lies to some other fools who
aren't free?
Because in this very place we are all treated the
same,
They're spoon feeding us pills thinking we all
can change,
Nothing matters to them; these faces just
scream insane.
Go ahead and take the few willing to dive down
below,
To those types of folks that think this is all just
a joke,
Even I fell victim to the evil this world provokes,
So, listen to how the poem goes, know what
means to stay woke.

GLASS HOUSE

As I have dreams,
        without borders
Aspirations
and beliefs held ever so tightly,
There are people that decided to cast their
stones upon my frail domain
Advertising their opinions so forcefully.
Yet, how quickly they are to forget about the
man who once had stones showered upon Him,
        for the beliefs He advocated.
And how later on He was able to cheat death,
        no,
        conquer death.
That man was judged
That man was ostracized
That man is who I believe in.
He gives me hope,
        justification,
        and immense strength.
I fortify my fortress
So, throw your stones,
for they are rendered useless.

SIZE 11s

Let us see if you can survive out in the ocean
the open abyss of emotions the closest thing
to a motive leaves me emotionless.
So, grab a paddle and I'll meet you at the end of
Knob Creek.
No, we will not be going for an 8-mile run but at
least walk a couple steps in my shoes to see
where I've come from.
Here is just a bunch of lowlife drunken stories
left for the next lonesome drunk to read from.
Let's just pretend like these strokes of ink are
lyrical stun guns.
Stay awake and stay alert
I am one with the discussion,
tell me what size you wear and yes, I'll even walk
a mile or two.
Even the bravest soldiers know
when the battle is
Absolute.

I SEE YOU

I see you
I hear you
I grew up with you
I've been in cuffs with you
I make music with you
I graduated with you
I will walk with you
I stand up with you
I've served with you
I will sit down with you
I raise my fist with you
I won't resist with you
I lost with you
I've been hurt with you
I fight with you
I live life with you
I share air with you
I will listen to you
I will respond to you
I will support you
I've celebrated with you
I work with you
I will eat with you
I will bleed with you
I will be better to you
I will not ignore you
I believe in you
I will change for you
I love you
I see you

THE GREEN ROOM

One step in front of the other
Come on
Keep walking,
     keep moving forward.
Have heart, time.

Breathe.
     Focus.
          Repeat.

No fear, only faith.
I talk to this rancid body of a man I call myself

Trying to control my heart rate from all the
adrenaline flowing out

The mountain of euphoria for which I sit upon
has given me a slight advantage to performing at
maximum potential

This is my passion
I'm about to share it with certain individuals
     With everyone
     With anyone
     With you

It's like I'm injecting a metaphorical super
potion into my system that makes me...
     Bulletproof,
     Untouchable,

human.

Past moments of being under extreme pressure,
My attempts have fallen short due to the lack of
self-confidence,

Dropping the ball was always my forte
Falling short of the finish line
Not measuring up to the challenge

I was welcome at
the table of delusion.

Anxiety levels maxed out, on the outside I'm
relaxed
You see; it was in that exact moment that the
man who I once was, tried to poke and pry his
way to the surface

Flooding my conscious with doubt
Casting away any certainty
Silencing my voice.

But not tonight....

No,
Not
tonight.
I own this night
It is my life.

GOD BLESS THE MUSIC

Picture this.
An illustrious day where music acted as an
antidote, not as a youthful phase,
Hip hop wasn't the game to be played,
It became the roots for our children's children to
understand how poets behaved.
How innovative thinking was displayed
Every genre had a purpose,
Every genre created brainstorms.
In modern day America, so called artists can't
even speak of any decent human traits,
No lessons to be learned,
        no reason behind the words,
                no motive behind the race.
Old dogs try to keep up with the new tricks
Rock n roll might slip off into the blue abyss
Bring back the past to the present and let us all
stand and deliver
Lovely lethal lyrics
Sound waves that act as a melodic therapy
The raw and provocative audio; blasting through
my headphones and consuming every tiny
atom that constructed my very being.
Paradise.
But not all music helps, overdoses happen with
many types of medication,
        There always will be noise and more noise
                evil escalates at all levels.
Even if there are good intensions

Sentences steaming on the back burner
So, when did the message be less important than
the rhythm or beat,
I mean why you care about the sound, if you
don't care about what people speak
To say the least, without words and movement
from
Tongues, jaws, cheeks and teeth, it won't get
others to think,
Maybe if we could enjoy the read, true music
wouldn't make our ears weep
Let us
Rescue the melodies

NOSTALGIC

I remember.
I remember the extent of my imagination as a
kid,
How eccentric it was and how it had no limits.
I remember it like it was yesterday.
I remember collecting Pokémon cards and
baseball cards and watching Batman on Saturday
mornings
I remember the joy of playing outside all day
until the streetlights turned on.
That was my curfew.
I remember the agony of rewinding a VHS tape
I remember being a young boy and wanting
nothing more than to grow up
I remember pulling all-nighters drinking a pack
of Red Bull, with my headphones blaring, while
downloading music off Lime-Wire.
I remember the days where I would be crawling
into bed from my bedroom window, at the same
time as my parents were making breakfast
Ahh, I remember that.
I remember cruising on the classy boardwalk of
Venice Beach, on a longboard, embracing
complete and
utter freedom.

I remember throwing bon fires in Oceanside and
falling asleep on the sand, only to be awaken by
the boys in blue.

I remember when my dad and I took a picture in front of the Twin Towers in New York, one week before the fall on 9/11.

Yes, I remember that well

I remember my 18th birthday and how that entire night seemed to be like a Hollywood movie script that was about to be the next blockbuster hit

It was crazy, wild, and strangely perfect.

I remember how those moments of constant bliss made me feel.

The feeling of; I don't know what I will be doing or where I'll end up, or If I was even going to make it home without being in handcuffs...but you know what? I felt ALIVE.

So alive that I chased those adrenaline highs for so long that I became a junkie.

I remember the fights my father and I had thinking this is just a phase, it'll pass, I'll be fine; but it didn't,

And no, I wasn't.

I remember exactly what I had for dinner on that cold Thursday night, where I became a poet.

I remember the insomnia, the living nightmares, the cold sweats, and the detox

I remember rehab, quite vividly.

I remember the exact moment when I realized the ugly truth to why I was an only child

Those were memories I wish I could forget.

But I remember how resilient this Scorpio has always been

Always finding some glimmer of hope in the darkest shadows.

I remember

I remember all the Yankees games, the L.A. road trips, the hotel parties and the concerts.
I remember starting a cypher in the middle of a sea of people, during Wu-Tang's set at Rock the Bells.
I remember how no one could ever take that experience away from me.
No one was more loyal to this type of lifestyle than yours truly.
I remember those nights oh too well.
I remember not seeing the face of my 1st son being born into this world because I was at boot camp.
But I do remember my second and my third son's birth, and that feeling simply cannot be described in words, not even by a novelist
I remember how my heart was beating out of my chest when I had to catch and kill a king cobra with my bare hands, in the Philippines
I remember it all.
I remember
I remember the site of all three of my boys playing in the snow for the first times of their lives.
That was a true image of tranquility.
I remember becoming a Christian
I remember the first time I jumped out of a helicopter.
I even remember the first night I walked up on stage, grabbing the mic for the first time ever and sharing my thoughts to a group of random people.

I remember how that made me feel.
I remember that power and what that adrenaline
did to me
I remember what writing with a pen in a
notebook feels like and how time stops and
nothing else matters, when you are in the zone.
Write it down quick before I hit that wall. You
know?
I remember, ohh man! How I remember!
I remember who I used to be and how different
that man was compared to who I am now
I remember looking back at my life and saying
wow it's been a hell of ride.
But I'm finally here now!
I remember what these words and phrases and
rhymes and metaphors and sentences meant to
me
I remember why I write
I remember being consumed by it all
Molded by it
I remember
and I will never forget.

THE POWER OF THREE

As the years go by
  only three reasons are proof to why I've
survived
My crazy yet intriguing life
  only has meaning due to my sons being alive
Young soldiers; don't cry
This one's for you, just in case daddy can't be
there by your side.
Read this for when I'm away
Read this for when you're in pain
Read this to calm your mind
  when the monsters come out to play.
Life is tough, Life is hard, but life is a blessing
So, remember, you always have each other to
conquer the world.
The immense love I have for you three; has no
end
And I will forever fight for you in any battle
given.
Evil will not know your names,
For I will be the one always standing in front of
its face.
As your father;
        I will never leave you,
        I will never give up on you,
        I will always support you,
        I will always protect you,
            And I will always love you.

My flesh and blood,
A mighty trio,
God speed.

ONE RAINY DAY

As the precipitation falls from the clouds
People look up into an abyss
The white and blue abyss gapping over the
crowds
We close our eyes
Wish and hope for the simple life
Gloom then covers our souls with grey
Because of this one rainy day
Under the rooftops we will stay

As puddles fill the cement
People walk past, splashing and clashing
With all of this time spent
Sons and daughters, all run inside
Trying to stay dry
Yet many love this feeling
The feel of being the only one out there
But how it won't stay, is just unfair

As we are drenched in the wetness
Our emotions intervene with this rain
And we are all senseless
Streets are overrun with this cold and
frightening fun
The rain is this in which
Why we stand outside just to be as one
Thinking subconsciously about the fields
The fields grow with the rain falling
Falling into the mouths, which keep on yawning

We look outside to this beautiful mirage
With our doors and windows all locked
It's like the little boy putting together a collage

Trees along with flowers just keep growing
Mother Nature drinks from the blue sky
And her garden of beauty keeps on showing

THE CALM BEFORE THE STORM

Deep beneath this slick sheet of skin, there is a
shade of blue
A contrast between empty thoughts and
unsolved clues
So, when you think falling to the ground is the
only way out
Stand up one more time and clear your mind of
doubt

Days go by as the wave's crash upon the shore
There are treasures underneath the sand, but I
don't know what they're for
Fluttered noises along with clustered voices now
fill my head
But if I make it through the night, I know I'll
soon be seeing red

Gathering the fittest like a soldier joining the
ranks
My vessel must be virile, or it'll be I who walks
the plank
Set the sails! Way anchor! It is time for our
voyage to begin
Our souls are at sea but courage, now that
comes from within

Look Captain! Steer Captain! For our ship will be
lost in the depths
I shout to my men, let us die with pride and to
be at peace with the rest,

Calypso has us at our throats, oh queen of the
sea, at least spare my crew
You see, my majesty, it is I who is the king of
this shipwrecked feud

At last, we hit land and all pain can be ignored
My regrets have been washed away and mind
has been restored

Section Two

The Darkness That Consumed

DIVINE CHAOS

Imagine
Divine chaos.
Life must be
harder than what comes
after all the lights vanish.

Some spend their days in fear,
of the moment they stare death in the face.
Counting the animals before they buy the farm.

We cannot curse at the wind for blowing away
the unwanted rubble
Dirt of this earth.

Death is intrinsic, unstoppable
It may not be what we want at times or maybe
we feel vengeful towards death
But there must be a correction to the
imperfection
Mayhem is managed
hysteria cannot be born from being afraid.

We must live life as if it is
                    Divine chaos.

NEED A TITLE FOR THIS SHIT

Turn down the music, shut the car   off
Loosen the grip on the steering wheel,
Slow down your thoughts   walk
Freeze them in time before they can ROT;
Rot
  Rot
    Rot away into the emptiness of your
consciousness

Move past the objects in your path that drive
you to the haunted abyss
That place where sunlight does not exist
Where the friends of black holes have an
abundance of doubt to cloud your bliss
I see no windows here
There are no doors
No life
No happiness
Only the ground and the walls are present.

The porcelain tile floor is cold and bleak
As toes curl with every step, they won't let me
get cold feet
I cannot leave.

Work here is strictly graveyard shifts
Pulling teeth with bleeding fingertips
Where insanity is a cure to what shadows
diagnose with

I struggle to sleep
Seek for companion
For my soul;

for it is beat.
But
Hope
Survives

And there is hope.

Even when all you want to do is drive off a cliff
into the sunset,
Forgetting about all your problems
                all your burdens
Bury yourself in that dark place
You cannot.

There is no magical road you can drive down,
that makes your stress and fears disappear
So, let that dark place only be a mirage in the
distance;
not a home.

            Say goodbye to that ride, pause
            Shout to the shadows, mock
            Keys in the ignition, lost.

JOKER'S DELIGHT

Saint or sinner
Tainted or pure.
I ask myself these questions quite often,
Which one of those am I more connected to,
who I am?
A saint full of sin?
Or a sinner in a saint's skin
The pessimist or the protagonist.

Wait, I'm more of a jester or a joker.
Due to my life consisting of a handful of bad
jokes
A semi-comedic messenger of uncanny
banters of humor and mischief.

Together we live in the present,
You and I.
With one foot in the shadows,
one arm raised to the sky,
Demonic vice grips, tightly grasping ahold of the
vessel as a squad of angels are pulling us away
Trying to save our souls from a cloak of evil
An earthly purgatory.
And unfortunately, our suffering isn't always
limited, right?
There is a thin line between embracing the
insanity
and flirting with rehabilitation
Again.

So, then we do what we have to do, to survive.

How can I foster comedy without it causing
permanent damage?
We both encounter the same problem
Funny, isn't it?
when simple smiling turns into sleek snickering
      Happiness turns into happy less
And the pursuit peaked at an unpleasant point
and plummets.
Slippery when wet you might say
Such a staggering slope to keep on the straight
and narrow

Now, you won't see me with greasy green hair
or a posse of crooked clowns
No deck of cards up my sleeve.

Let's use laughter as a coping mechanism,
a humorous shield
fending off the waves of depression and pain.

Laughing now and laughing tomorrow
Our actions aren't to amuse others,
Don't be afraid of the opening act.

I call myself a joker,
Because I've never learned how to take off this
mask.

THE CROW

Every diluted day
I stare through these dark brown iris windows
Only to come face to face with reality
Struggling with the norm,
       I don't fit in.
A misguided crow, if you may, flying below an
arc of doves
Searching, for food
          And recognition.
With no absolute destination,
I am undesignated
Disturbed
Marking myself as a dark soul.
Subsequently,
Similar symptoms have been diagnosed to those
whose agendas
Were labeled insane.
And...
I've never been one to follow the crowd,
       Mud-stained clothes plagued my wardrobe.
Sooner or later,
My flaws will render me flightless,
       Uninvolved with the murder
Yet I will still exist from within.

In life or death,
I am who I have always been, No change.
  No branch of green shrubs can stop this
flood

Or temper the storm.
So, I must be able to see, the other birds,
To quietly document the actions and habits of
the ones who make their presence known.

Carefully copying and studying how to apply the
camouflage.
Altering an image that is to be reflected
And this crow; will not be one to hold a grudge.
Scouts honor.
I learn patience, become content with the way
people continue to spray
 blackened sin,
 throughout this Earth.
 Caw caw caw, cancer
 How many have tried to erase their mistakes
that were etched in stone?
 What does it take to plant a rose where the
weeds have grown?
 Maybe I should have been a dove,
            instead of the crow.

WITHIN IN WARD

In every song scream out loud with every breath
Nothing will ever stop me not even death
In life we'll never know what lies in front of us
So, leave those ugly memories within the dust

Within the ward there is a key
Every night I ask myself why
Why did I never just let things be?
Within the dust there is a dime
Found it not knowing its value
Its purpose or its place in time
Within the dust there is a nail
I pick up and realize how it makes me feel
Brain dead and skin pale

I write these chronicles to find if I'm alone
To see if someone out there feels the same
Someone out there to welcome me home
Everything on this earth isn't always so clear
It's the demons within the dust that I fear

Within the ward there is a hand
Pulling it out of its misery
I help bring up a troubled man
Within the ward there is a faint cry
The man questions his place on this earth
I ask myself the same question, why?
Within the dust there is a pen
It's filled with my human blood
He pushes forth the death note, asking me when

Within the dust I find that He is here
That thing lives with me and in every inch
Trying and trying to make him disappear

A REFLECTION NOT A SELF IMAGE

When I stare into the mirror
    I see this carbon copy
Of a man with an oddly shaped smile
    And a single tear running down the side of
his cheek
Ever so slightly, shaking.
I can hear his thoughts,
As if they are my own.
      Facial expressions could be fake
      And core feelings aren't relevant
Does he feel lost in a narcissistic world with the
intentions of making a difference
or is he just lost?
He's studying the face of the man
that is looking back at him
As I am doing the same.
Puzzled.
Wondering, am I truly living in this so-called
reality?
Is this really what the rest of the world sees

Why are all mirrored images reversed?
Raising my left arm,
    as he raises his right,

But both fists clenched
Is there a small glimpse of madness?
mistakenly displayed by the pain reflecting off
of the irises?

Or is it a hallucination...

Those dark
Brown
Eyes.

Don't try to understand,
Those eyes tell a story that no man can unveil
It's a whisper spoken in the wind
A secret
Between me and
My reflection.

SEMI-COMATOSE

Sounds are faint, my hearing is damaged
Even looking back at what I've done, I am
pleased.
As my eyesight is dim,
I am found.
My hands have gone numb
Trying to hold a balance.
                 in an unbalanced world.
I am not to bailout when the chips are down
Look at this place, look at it only as a noun
I've packed my packs ready to leave town.
Take a drag,
       Take a breath,
             Kiss me.
Go beyond these simple complexities
See to why bread can't go without butter
Recycle any thoughts of happiness to use at
later dates
Start pulling the covers, daylight fades
As the angel of death keeps her promise,
I struggle to stay asleep
I guess it's just the fight in me,
Lord; take me home.

MY DRUG

I've done things some will never think to do
Overcame obstacles, not knowing if I'd make it
through
It's made me something that I'm not proud of
You've turned into something I've had to love

As I now know the measurements and weight
Staring at my unsteady hands
Knowing this was never part of my fate

Living a lie becomes one with this pain
Because of this world, my world will never be
the same
An addiction is a force stronger than self will
And it's this force that I'm unable to kill

Inhaling the fumes that continue to linger on
Is how my inner addict tries to stay calm?
So, I feel the want and accept the need
But will never give in, breaking my creed

The aftershock breaks me down to a point of no
return
The night was young as I emerged
I guess brain cell count was none on my concern

There are many past sins that I've loved to
commit
This story is about my drug and whether or not I
should quit...

REHAB

The night seemed bleak as we emerged in the
rain
Standing at the doorway of a building
With no name
Not knowing where to go,
               where to sleep,
                    benign and unclean.
How did I let the disease consume me and run
me up the walls?
Now I'm stuck in a room where time stalls,
                  and my skin crawls
I walked on the dark side of the dark side of the
moon, thinking I was bulletproof
No, I'm not injured, my dear, but I do need
medical help
Do you know why?
          I'm ashamed to tell you.
          I'm ashamed of what I've kept hidden.
All I have at this point is wishes, hopes, and
dreams
Lying in a bed I've made as I have plagued its
sheets
Baby, don't let me go
Don't let me be
I got this, it's all on me.

SOBER

Look at yourself and see what you need
Tell me if it matches with what you believe
Then I'll try to understand
I've been lost without answers for years
It's like I blame others yet staring into a mirror
My reflections aren't helping me none

Sitting on the curb with a broken heart
Will show the world how a man can be hurt
And still look like a fool right from the start
Even then he wouldn't dare look for fortune or
fame
Having the will to live on in fear
Can damage the life he once rightfully claimed

The shadows of my past cloud my thoughts
As they keep baring down on my shoulders
Life becomes one great big knot

Barren wastelands now call my name
I answer to them
Completely consumed by shame

I ANSWER THEM YET REMAIN NAMELESS

The shadows are calling
those cunning shifty shadows are calling
            and once again,
        I become who they answer to
They taunt me.
They come around when the chips are down
When the fuel gauge is low
When my self-esteem is nonexistent.
                "Hey there son," they cry out,
"Do you remember who we are?
We coddled your broken insignificant body as
you faked a frown throughout that meaningless
so called
life you once thought you lived.
We were there.
You don't remember us?
I know you felt our...presence...
Don't you remember when you were so high and
feeling extremely depressed, that you thought it
was easier to exist in reality when you escaped
it?
Do you remember who was there to help you
coax with,
The anger issues,
The laws you broke
Those countless holes in bedroom doors and
walls,
and the broken bottles

What about all your adolescent problems...?
(Chuckles)

Who was there when you wrestled with alcohol
and drugs and the indecisions birthed from
panic and
curiosity?
Come on
Come back and stand with us just for a little
while
because we remember.
We were there.
You cast us out and say that WE were the
disease? (Chuckles)
   We were your fucking safety net, Soldier."
     silence
Damn.
Those words acted as microscopic knives that
pierced deep into my ear drums
.... with such deception....so sinister...
I swished those verses through and through
Every word
Some words even turned on me as they were my
comrades now wanting me to walk the plank...
Brainstorm category 666
But...
My answer
It all came down to what my answer was.
What I was going to do next.
My answer wasn't profound or earth shattering
It just had meaning, it held truth behind it
It was unsettling but quite intriguing

I answered those whispers in the dark in such a
way, even I was surprised

I said,
"NO! I am my own cancer. "
And walked away.

...They had no power over me.
(Those) were the words that were loyal to me
and the breath was worth wasting.
I liked being a sick minded individual
But I am still cognizant
When I laugh, they get frustrated
When I cry, they think I'm weak
When I struggle, they turned their backs
When I succeed, they orchestrate
They hate what I've become.
But there is one thing I am that they are not
I am human.
Flesh and bones.
Too bad for them.
I win.

MR. FEAR

Today I saw a man that looked at me with a
slimy faint grin,
As I walked near him,
I noticed his eyes had a shiny green tint.
Fresh gusts of wind blew back his jacket that
was black as sin
There was a feeling at first that made me think,
is this something I've felt before?

In a state of paranoia, I knew this feeling was
something I could not ignore,
Pacing back and forth, listening to every voice in
my head till there was no remorse.

I finally stopped and stared into those eyes and
said, "I guess it's just my time,"
The man laughed at me, and replied, "
I'm something that lives inside"

And just like that he disappeared off to
somewhere in Shanghai.
I thought it was weird at first, as the adrenaline
started to die down,
If it wasn't my time to fly what does the morning
have in store when I lay down?
Should I count my blessings or should I look up
to the sky crying out.

The night was bleak when a couple of grey
clouds gave me a little something to drink
Walking down that empty street wondering if
that man was real, real enough to speak

He kinda looked like me, but I'm confused about

what he said, and what he meant?
Slowly I began to wonder,
Was that the fear talking?
or a figment of my dreams?

BARELY A MAN

A man was just broken with sadness
He was a man who thought nothing was fake
But the one thing that beat him, was fate
All the tracks lead back to his mistakes
He learned from others but not himself
That's how his feelings ended up on a shelf

A man was blinded with fear
Didn't have the courage to face you
Never knew the beauty of them two
He couldn't contemplate the harm
The damage was done to him the night of
They were never ever ready for any love

Now he tells me why he can't be a man
She took his heart and ripped it in two
For how she never cared, he always knew
All this thoughts and outlooks on life were
tattered
Needed something to live for
She was now gone and never wanted more
This man never saw it coming
This man couldn't be let down easily
This man was of course, a fiend

He stuck a knife to his heart
Didn't know the amount of pain
Started to weep as it started to rain
His heart was a ticking time bomb
The bomb was set and ready to explode
He set his mind to 'for better or worse' mode

The streets stood in place with no names

He wasn't looking for no fortune, no fame
He was only looking for her
His feet dragged through the streets he walked
on
His heart not sure where it would belong
The streets are now his home, and this man is
alone

This man never saw it coming...
This man was broken and beat down
This man always was so loving...
This man is never to be found

TRUE ABUSE

As days fly past
I wonder if life lasts
The way I want it to
As the sun sets
Rights are what I forget
Have nothing to get me through
Now a dead man
Tells me to strongly stand
And to find a clue
This isn't who I am
Obeying every coward's command
I'm blind in this noose
Heart full of pain
I wonder if I'm insane
Can you tell me the truth?
Consisting of crazy chains
This life I have made
Misery shows false proof
Writing feelings on paper
Friends seem to think they're creators
Do I look like a fool?
Save scissors for later
Killing cells with a stapler
I've been played like a tool
No beat to any drums
Realizing what I've done
Beautiful blades begin the abuse
Laughing but having no fun

A monster is what I've truly become
I really have been used

WHY ME?

Show me something great I can become
Because of the man I've been
hates the amount of shit I've done
Leave my thoughts and feelings behind
can't show you a definite change
I still need to find a reason why

The countless mistakes roll around the skull too
much
I have the feeling of what I want but it hurts to
touch
Don't mind me, I won't be here for long
just rest in peace listening to my song

Thinking that you're fitting in with the world
can always change and confuse the mind
Knowing the difference between fake and for
real
That's the answer I'm going to find

I hate you, I do, but I will not leave
Never try to translate my thoughts
My own being will construct life very well and
keen
Lying all the time, you cheat, you are a witch
You screwed up my life once
Now it's nothing I will leave you with

It began as though we both thought as one

We argued so much we didn't have any fun
You thought you were always so damn perfect,
the one for me
Truth is, I never wrote you a song, I just let the
ink bleed

As my hand writes this small poem
I doubt myself and wonder why
How am I happy standing alone?
With a pair of wings unable to fly

SECRETS

Sitting here with chaos cluttered confines
My life is destined for a decline
Unsure of how my future will turn out to be
An altercation ending in an awe of agony

I'm just a fragment falling from faithful fears
There's absolutely nothing wanted to keep here
The excuses are exceeded far beyond my lies
I've yet to bring myself together
To act upon every opinion, I have antagonized

The world once made total sense to me
Starting to lose grip of success
And question happiness among all humanity
So, I now wait for whatever comes next
Hoping to dwell in my dreams
And teach my secrets to subjects

Born and raised in a place with different faiths
I embellish my anger and hide behind hates
The secrets in these poems cannot be taught
Too complex to completely understand
Harsh words that will make your brain rot

Clearing my head in search of some clarity
Luck can never be placed in prosperity
But if your fortune faces an irrefutable feeling
It's understood that you're still a human being

As my writings are shrouded secrets within words
A life-threatening altercation has yet to occur

FAKE FEELINGS

You walked into my life without a clue
But for what the following had put us through
We ended up in each other's arms

These lonely days without you will be something
I can't stand
I want you to hold me close and squeeze my
hand
Let this time together always fill your veins
Fill it up like my ink does to each page

Without you
Without us
Without life
Without lust

We didn't waste any time at all, we chased and
chased
But in order to be the next Bonny & Clyde
It needed to be us, two perfect people face to
face
Laughing and blanking out, yet thanking fate
As the night shuts out the day
I out stretch my arms but are seconds too late

Why can't I have an angel?

She needs me to feel her sweet, soft arms
I look up to the sky to see if God knows
How horrible the scent of her stings my nose

REASSURANCE

As you pierce the skin, the love drops out
Black in dismay, my head filled with doubt
Pick up this blade realizing the disaster
Crushing my heart faster and faster

It takes forever hours to register in my brain
Convincing this body that's not insane
It takes forever hours to register in my brain
Convincing my family that I'm not insane

Bleeding scars remind me of the shadow of my
past
Not knowing where the scrutiny will lead
I rapidly follow someone else's footsteps
To find a place to sleep
Let's fake these feelings, who cares anyway
Don't cloud my thoughts
My soul can't accept what you say

Never have I had this pen as my weapon of
choice
You stabbed it till it bled
Because of what you have heard from my blank
voice

I was loyal right till the very, bloody end
Now it's my scabbed heart that I'll have to lend

UNBALANCED BEAUTY

Don't be surprised if I never reappear
Fighting through the darkness and shattered
glass
Doubting myself being afraid of its fear

Deep inside this beautiful yet broken body
Lays a secret no living creature can see
They've made it a tumor on dying tissue
It's a pointless fight on worthless issues
And I've been chosen once again

You have released a new demon in me
I don't have to agree so now, just flee
Distance yourself and die in the dirt
You used knives and words that make the hurt
This thing called life, we can't take a second look
I'm not through with you, you better stay
And give back these dreams that you took

Dig into your chest, pull out your heart
To see if I have made my wretched mark
Never laugh at another man's downfall
Or people won't see you live long at all
I've consumed the new black to cover my grey
Hating the life, I've been given
It's all I have so I've decided to stay

New laws created by my greater power
Telling me, I'm nothing but a silly coward

But I'm not, I stand tall at the edge
Never falling down, never looking back
Revenge is relief and that's one true fact

So, stay hand in hand with compassion and
grace
As the devil dances over many lands of lies
He leaves out the truth while influencing
mistakes
A worthy opponent who never wins a prize

FOOL ME TWICE

Wipe the beloved memories from the mind
It's the hate we had that will be left behind
Pieces of a broken heart are all we could find
To truly understand me, you had to have seen
the signs

The thought of you enables my eyes to open and
see
Due to the anguish and misery that lies
underneath
Slitting my own throat sounds pretty appealing
to me
Here we who go to dwell with the devil's deceit

Your scent always made my muscles and nerves
relax
Let my guard down, stepping straight into a trap
Was it my fault or just another devil's dance?
I will never know because you didn't give me a
chance

As my instincts scratch and scream at my own
sorrow
You're now alone on that path I've refused to
follow
Simply stuck in yesterday's wishing I never saw
tomorrow
Writing this suicide note because my heart is
now hollow

Why did you have to tell me your true feelings?
Just for them to develop a harsh and
hypothetical healing

So, as I break off a part of my being
The devil whispers wise words that manipulate
the meaning

To defy the dead and decompose all of my
depression
Altering my anger must become an oblique
obsession
Slicing my wrists prove I feel no pain
That's how you think when you've lost the game

Now having so much hate, the devil becomes my
friend
I don't want this broken heart to mend
Because it feels ethical to be angry once again

DEFYING GRAVITY

This is gonna be up front and personal, not a
view from the cheap seats
Waterlines rising, I'm feeling like it's knee
deep
My anxiety is steadily creeping, and I can't
sleep
I've been down this same road without a
grand scheme,
While throwing other priorities in the back
seat.
I'm ashamed of who's in the rear view-he's
staring back at me
We are driving this whack machine like we're
on some combat action team
Not a care in the world about my mental
state, this ain't Assassins Creed
I can't restart my life and respond, due to
some broken dreams and shattered peace,
I'm not the master thief
Wars waging inside of me and I'm tired of
being a casualty
That's the version of myself that's actually
living unhappily
They say the games a marathon not sprints,
And I've always been tardy to track meets
Been a student to this type of lifestyle-but
never part of the faculty.

So, I don't need to blast a beat alongside my crafty speech,
Because then the message might whiz right past your cheeks
And so, what if I got a bad rap sheet
I'm still here, damnit,
Determined to have a bright smile and defy gravity.

DON'T FORGET ME

Times have been hard; times will never be the
same
Life's too short so promise you'll remember me
Remember me for what I do
I don't like saying goodbye
I don't like life, but I'll always love the sun

This world has turned its back too many times
I just need to know your surviving
Need to know what you're into, what you still
like
Need to know how you truly feel
You've always been the one they read in my
poems
And how it's my heart you've happened to steal

To me words are nothing without pens and
paper
It's just how my thoughts are understood
Thoughts of you creep in my mind everyday
Thoughts of us always make my heart shrink
Dreamed of how we'd always be at each other's
side
Past memories, oh how they make me think

CONTROLLING MY FATE

Everything I had
Everything that I ever owned
Was all lost on a dark, dreadful day
A place I once called home

Pacing by the window
Unknown of the torment I would see
Angered by the sin flow
Her presence stained the front seat

A different type of pain has now emerged
Ready to give it my all
To find the one thing that lost its worth
I understand now that happiness isn't far away
The edge comes quick
When your confidence is made of clay

This man, this creature knows his own fate
Pulling the dull out of the light
Trying to find his direction
Questioning himself what to do to fight

At a sudden moment, experiences seemed
familiar
Yet, knowing this heart hasn't picked the best
streets
Buried this body of lies into the deep
And prepared me to strengthen the weak

There is nothing left except for what we know
All these memories are to be shattered
And to finally,
have his name left to be unknown

THE RUNAWAY

I'm troubled by trust, mistakes are accused of
being mine
No need to rush...I'm just running, running away
from time
Strip my bed of scarring sins, I can't sleep
tonight
No need for pills...my heads screwed, screwed
on too tight

If I leave my home and never look back
People will start to worry, and I'll just laugh
Burning memories, forgetting the past
Questioning life, constructing the contrast

Living in color, bleeding forever red and black
Deep down within my own heart
Is that needle, found in your haystack?

Physically, closing my mouth for I am insane
Poetically, searching for a life full of fame

The way down this lonely and God-forsaken
Road
Shall be walked in wrath and the one I chose
Blackening doubt, explaining the tone
Demanding courage, remembering that I'm alone

Losing to misery, men can cry and moan
Life leads us to believe lies
That is why, my life's a complex poem

Hypothetically, if you were asked to come with,
Hopefully, it is me that you will miss

Risk has rescued me, I am The Runaway

METANOIA

No matter the size of the scabs,
No matter the height of the fall,
You can't outrun your past,
It catches up to us all.

Somehow, something crawled into my mind
It got past my defenses,
Got past the henchmen,
And shattered my front line.
Sometime, somewhere staring at the bottom of a
bottle,
Wasn't going to be suffice,
Only made emotions collide,
And glued my foot to the throttle.

Even when I wanted to slow down,
That's when I started hearing, "It's over now!"
You can't stop a train from crashing when
someone cuts the brakes,
You can't expect someone to love vastly when
their happiness is erased.
In so many instances when I was young,
My father told me, "You'll understand when
you're older, just go out and have fun..."
It was the only decent advice he ever gave me
Because when I'm alone and angry,
I think of that boy wanting to grow up to live
this life,
Where all a man does is just fight,

wanting to go back and tell that boy, to just stop
But we can't pick the morale of our own story,
We can only picture the plot.

I walk a line so thin; you might say I have my
own circus act
I can't tell you how I got here,
I can't tell you where it started,
But I can draw you a pretty screwed up map.
There's a kink in my DNA,
A broken link in my chains,
I find ways to ruin sure things,
And let others suffer with continuous pain.

I write these pages to keep my inner demons
inside
Voices telling me to step back into the darkness
Will never see another glimpse of light
Will never truly own my life

BLIND IN THIS BLUE

Can't see anything, there's nothing at the front
Can't hear a thing so I try to speak
Nothing is as real as it was before
As all of our mouths just hit the floor

Lungs long for a lonely tune
Can't stop to think of what's caught in nets
Stay blind in this blue
But don't dare to shut these eyes
Because with this pen there will still be light

Feel the world around yet still bleak
Cover these blind eyes but still try to speak
You've shown how and left out the rest
Ripping out what's grown from the sockets
Letting the blood bleed down to the chest

There's no way to truly look into your eyes
No reason or voice behind lies
No block to stop this demise
No present along with a surprise
Just can't help that,
...lungs are listening for a tune
   Eyes aren't searching for anything new
   Still blind in this blue
   still trying to save everything about you.

QUARANTINE

Altered, without apathy
Questions stirring of what's to come

As we pick up the pieces of a shattered image or
a beautiful memory.
that once was whole.

The corners become tattered,
They start to display that time is real
They peal back a little bit, exposing the multiple
layers that exist,
Hidden from the naked eye
Limiting it to be able to fit together the way it
once did.

We try to replace what we lost
Maybe by looking around for different pieces
that could click into place
Ones that are similarly shaped

But they don't.

Even when you know deep below the surface
that there's something missing,
something that has been broken,
There's nothing to fill that void
No forward progression
Feeding the flame with premium gasoline,
not water
its human nature.
Casting the first of many stones could lead
to an avalanche, of regret
in certain instances,

When something has died, there will never be
replacement
No vacancy
Only anguish

HELLO FATHER

Hello, father how have you been?
I remember your face, yet I still carry your sin
Hello, father how have you been?
When was the last time you have seen my kids?
Hello, father how have you been?
I never seemed to forget all the things you did
Hello, father how have you been?
Why are you still living underneath my skin?

You're the reason why I'm so afraid of failure
Being right was more important than being a
savior
Wasn't I worth fighting for?

Hello, father what have you done?
I may be blood, but I am not your son
Hello, father what have you done?
Do you even remember when we actually had
fun?
Hello, father what have you done?
They called me a disgrace and you left me so
numb
Hello, father what have you done?
Are you really surprised with how I've become?

There's a void in my heart where the love for a
father should be
I will never be the same because of how you
betrayed my family
Do you really always have to be right?

Goodbye, father I'll be seeing you again

Was there some place better that you had to
attend?

Goodbye, father I'll be seeing you again
I can't even trust you to act as my friend
Goodbye, father I'll be seeing you again
Maybe someday my life will be worth your
defense

ONLY BY BLOOD, NOT BY CHOICE

Everyday seems as if I'm at the edge
Voices telling me to jump, flow through my head
You keep living your life, yelling at me
Can't find that equal balance
To why the pain has cut so deep

I've clenched my fists in anger too many times
You had the chance to change but ignored the
signs
Controlling obsessively a rebel of a son
Is it worth it all, or has your reign just begun?

Let's see what you've got, I know you're cheap
I'll play your games as I grind my teeth
So just break me down, beat me to a pulp
Don't be content with my fears, it wasn't my
fault

My past regrets match this present rage
But if our relationship won't ever change
I have pens and paper to be my escape

Just so you know, the man you claim to have
raised
Now speaks of you as the hardest obstacle he's
faced

DERANGED AND PLEASURES

Every day is so hard to understand
Sometimes it feels like it has a motive
Others don't go according as planned
Deranged pleasures
That's just what the world's cut out to be

Where is the root of this disease?
Thought I was the cure, but this is killing me
Thought you saw me as the reason
Erase all the effects to set me free

I feel anger taking hold
Afraid of the lies that I have sold
Tore my eyes out, not able to see
I now dwell with insanity
Consume the black, I can't deny it anymore

Divided thoughts,
Under a cloud of dust
Developing the cause
From what I touch
Deranged, not pleasured

THE KILLER IS A WITNESS

Tell me if the world is worth an arm and leg
The life I put on paper describes false fate
As you search the unknown and question
yourself
I choke and wonder about these feelings I've felt

The words spoken shook me exceedingly hard
Wasn't expecting a single heartbeat
Excepting my excuse of doubt and disregard

Since the anger seethe your blood from the
thought
Countless times of how I lead to let down
Be a witness to my heart being ripe to rot
Although acting but yet never faking a frown
Ripping out my tongue, unable to talk
God has left me a limb of an unsound

Open up wide, the truth is hard to take
Especially since it could be unreal
So, ask yourself if you are authentically awake

Don't let this bit of ink be harsh, accept the
therapy
It's a way of helping to a certain degree
I know where I belong, dwelling in the dark
Because there is no life left in my heart

Don't let a gun be the solution to curing your
head
Don't let me be alone to think I'm better off dead

CEASE OF CONFLICTS

Looking down as your head is in my hands
I dropped you down but couldn't break away
My head's telling me to drag you home
But my heart's not letting me stay

My eyes stare at the blood running to the gutter
I hear all the sirens and whys
Searching for a reply, all I can do is stutter
All the masses seize to stop and listen to
This sound of a dying heartbeat
Which is a cry that is long overdue

I feel the rage build up inside
Tearing from the middle, my arms outstretched
wide
My heart has never been something to hide
Because I now hold something that couldn't
survive

Having our heads against one another
Your distant memories flush out my brigade
They see no tears fall from my face
Because of the game you played

My efforts were never enough, you were never
mine
Let's start from day one, to understand what we
see
I was only the shoulder to cry on

As a light turns on inside, the answer is clear to
me

Boiling tensions are one with scarred wrists

It's a combination I never thought to mix Pull up
the curtain, explain your tricks
Your death is a cease to all our conflicts

The night is chemo-clear, you were only my
cancer
I injected you into my life
My misery will now act as an enhancer

SILENT CRAZE

Different things go round and round in my head
It's nothing new it's just simple brain damage
I'm wounded but yet still am standing
I don't need help it's nothing I can't manage

No-one really knows what's going on in my mind
You all will be shocked by what you find
Seeing your face drowning in dismay and disbelief
It's these secrets you saw from the underneath
Questions become nothing going in one ear and
seeping through
No-one can understand who I really am
Everyone only judges what they say I do

A silent chariot rides through my lands as a plague
Cut the hair on my scalp beginning to shave
This dig is one that I can't stop
Afraid of revealing something I am not

Now scratching away and peeling off my skin
Hearing footsteps leading to something
I can't grasp on, it's somewhere I haven't been

As I swim in the pool of betrayal
Glimpses of light track me down
And the minute I go under
It's my heart at the bottom that I've found

No time for forgiveness no time for regret

I unraveled the man I am today
And won't tell all the secrets I've kept
Dreaming of the day I find a key to my skull
The skin is gone I've hit the bone
I've dug nothing but a deep dark hole

BLACKENED REMAINS

You don't understand what you did to me
You can't see the damage, it's all underneath
You told me things no one else would ever know
You are the reason why these feelings flow
You never walked a mile over my troubles
enough to see
...All of things I had to do to stop the bleed

I was just a boy who walked that mile
I was so stupid to love your cunning smile
I only spoke to you apart from the rest
I now know that you could have cared less
I have taken you out of my life, you are not
welcome here
...All is said and done, you are dead to me, my
dear

Started to cry out and shatter my right lung
The stakes were set too high, I've already won
Come on and tell me who we should blame
Ink pens and rusty knives won't ever look at me
the same
Because you broke me down and twisted my
gears
Thought I was nothing, so I disappeared
Maybe we'll meet again sometime soon
The lonely sun has to survive without its moon

My depth perception is getting weak

Your heart isn't like my own, it's so unique
I stab it once, twice, can't seem to cut the veins
Still digging a hole finding these black remains

So, shield my heart and mobilize my soul
Let nothing enter my gates
And still love the world as a whole

WALKING IN THE DARK

I'm still in your life but I'm never there
It wasn't my decision you just didn't care
Street signs act as if everything is the same
I only can hope the colors and names changed

Where I end up, will be some place unknown
But at least I know where I can from
So, I will always find my way back home

Scars and bruises are trophies to my own shame
I've seen these streets in many days of light
You might think you have stolen my fear
But you left one soldier out there for a fight

Shadows overcome the lights by which they
were under
They constantly call my name and laugh
It's to them that I will never surrender

Tell me why we walk around staring at the moon
Ask yourself why you can't close your eyes
It's the darkness that consumes you
And it's me who's made you believe my lies

"A creature of darkness can still have light in his soul."

OPEN WATER

Days are always so vivid and blue
Just as a rock falling from a cliff
I'm falling pretty hard for you
Oh no it's happening once again
Can't stand the moment when you leave
These deep feelings come from within

The storm that I survived, wadding through
Harsh conditions gave me a stronger clue
So come on and be my star in the sky
Don't close your eyes
Just please promise me that you'll stay alive

Swimming to the nearest thing to grab on to
My whole life I've never found this thing
I've always been alone and so cold
But remembering that it's always been on me
Pulling through all the cargo and nets
Trying so damn hard to become free
The weight of my mind keeps me from the
surface
Not knowing if I'll lose my breath
Yet I keep fighting to find my own purpose

The next sunrise, I'll stand tall with hands at my
side
The next full moon, I'll know I lost nothing but
my pride
I'm the one to blame for this nosedive

Wash off the fears
Wipe up the sweat
The waters just right

AN ANONYMOUS ANSWER

Trying to withstand this rotten fall
Meaningful memories are what's hard to recall
It's the unfortunate that seem to stick

Happiness can never continue to stand by
Seems to disappear when times are unsteady
So, share the secret to an ordinary life

When we ponder thoughts of being human
Due to certain fumes, we breathe
Realizing now the deception is only the bed
These emotions are what is keeping us dead
Burning spirit through and through

Trust is a problem that exists in mad minds
The reason to why there is misery to find
Afraid of letting an analyst read between my
lines

Self-inflicting pain are results of the unguarded
Weakness in the heart is how this got started
Trying to unlock an answer without the key
By staring at these walls unknowingly

The day life leaks the fluid of the soul
Defiance will drain it up to fill this hole
And bring broken knees up once again

SHADOW OF THE PAST

Just as the winds of apathy flow through my
mind
The reasons to why I need to question are so
hard to find
I'm always searching for an answer to problem
that lies within
A region of my reality that hasn't had a chance
to begin

The dust on my gears has enabled me from
walking
But the wetness from my tears hasn't enabled
me from talking
You see, love itself is an imperfect concept
An utterly miserable piece of a person's life
conquest

Yes, I surely have stepped off my crooked yet
chaotic path
It just so happens that I consumed myself with
too much wrath
My right hand was strong, steady but also badly
scarred
They say ugly memories never fade but bad
habits die hard

So, with a leap of faith and a fist full of sweat
I will always remember my mistakes but never
have regrets

FACES IN THE CROWD

Do you see my face?
I see others

Reflections barely reflecting, anything

So, where's the centerpiece?
Centerfolds are missing
They're images
of uncertainty
Unwanted
Longing for attention
Longing to be enough
Do you hate what I used to be?
        Or love what I've become
Notebooks of old pictures, snap shots
        time capsules
        photography
Every instrument used, to grasp the moments of
happiness,
Discernment or any other emotions

In a form where we can touch and hold
and feel.

Awaiting to be forgotten or thrown away.
We take our portraits
The self-imagery, for granted.

I'm sorry son, you keep on smiling
your face will be noticed

An appealing appearance
Without documentation

Soon enough,
They will see you.

THE CRASH

To the end of my mind and back
Failing to sift through my sin
Don't ask me who I am
I'm still trying to figure out where I've been
Settling on the back burner
Never thought I was meant to grow older
Moved away from the heat, just as my life grew colder
Been walking so long with the weight on my shoulders
Of why I am no longer in the passenger seat
So, fight for something you have strived for,
              more than just a soul
Blinked twice and lost control,
              fled the scene after it rolled

Constantly calling for help with no mercy
Blaming others but not myself, am I worthy?
Questions appear as answers
Being different is such a disorder
Now I see what's in front of me, is it reality?
Is it possible to create a self-image, or just a reflection?
My mistakes are so automated
But all I really need to know is why
Why has my life been reversed instead of in drive?
Death will soon destroy all the demise
Speed versus velocity

Knowledge versus experience
So, no matter what road we are on, what lights
we speed through
It's the crash that changes us

SPLENDID MISERY

As I start washing the waste from my mind
Nothing belonging to me can stay, just lies
Meaningless memories can't seem to detach
from my skull
loving the life, I used to have
Still waiting for this splendid misery to leave a
mark on my soul

Retracing my steps to see what I have done
Corruption is calling for what this place has
become

For every single hated moment, curse the
damned
Can't accept the true meaning to who you are
So, you gave into greed and plagued this land
So many strings of sorrow pierce the strongest
shields
Can't go on living this way
Save myself now and move beyond the distant
fields

Realizing reasons to how my heart beats even
faster
Compassion is calling me to be the places'
master

Seeking for wealth not for fame but distributing
the cost

At one point we lose faith in ourselves
Yet the blood that's been drawn is still blood
lost
My birthplace has always given me the cold

shoulder
Yet never have I turned my back

For fear feeds on the feeble as we grow older

INNER DEMONS

On this certain Sunday
In many testaments I will dwell
As we run to go and tell
them of what has happened
I cut out my heart
And slit their throats
Take their money
And see if their bodies can float
This rebellion begins with blood shed
To be born again
I must get out of my head

Linger upon my distant courage
Stay with me till death, so freedom can emerge
Let us fight for what we need
Kill the demons within
And wash our sins in the deep
I am not afraid of dying
I am not afraid to choose
I am afraid of this world
And what I have to lose

Dig deep into the minds of the inferno
Howl into the night to make the internals quake
Let this night continue with fright
And think if this is safe to partake

I do not know what day I shall die
Live without any burden, without sin

Burn the alter on which I fall
Having these inner demons never consume me
again

A TRIBUTE TO AGONY

You took me for granted and thought I'd be fine
Walking the many miles grasping for an
unlettered sign
Through every piercing profane word, for every
tiny toxic tear
I questioned what the outcome would be
Who exactly was that man staring back at me?

Never giving up on hate, we were constantly
confused
Even then trying to control the darkest shades of
love
You'll eventually see I was the assistant of an
accused

Fisted hands of fear tightened the rope
By which our beginning skims the surface
Always carrying a heavy load of hope

Collecting all the lies
The reason is revealed
Expecting to destroy my demise
Our thoughts will be concealed
Without sight, without sound, humbly
hardheaded
For our vows will be announced
And the love won't stop, until we reach the
clouds

Lost in my own faith, my face turning a
boisterous blue
Our relationship shall forever be inalterable
For this tribute to agony, I put my whole life
into.

In a dying moment of inhaling your last cigarette
I beg for your forgiveness and love
Since all of my scars are starting to collect

As my blood shot eyes turn to shiny white cues
I hope a chance with me is one you'll choose

FACE TO FACE

The day was cold, and the night was young
Shadows can't match what masks can make men
become
He could feel the crisp air brush across his
rugged hands
As the sun was getting its last glance at our
rancid lands.

When twisted thoughts meet an innocent mind
A man's intentions to be someone he's not,
Turn into an awe of sublime.
An unhinged idea starts to subdue daily
routines, a front is formed
His eyes can't truly see what his untamed palms
touch to shield the storm

A relentless amount of hope stirred constantly
inside his mentality
He fostered his own way to deal with demons,
lurking in reality
They say to him; "hello there friend, you are not
alone but we come with a price
Imagine your words written in books, imagine
your name up in lights...
Our bargain comes with a plague upon your life,
sleeping in filth on a bed of lice."
The man smiled, shaking his head from East to
West, once or twice

No amount of pain could equal to what these
creatures had in store
The man had to protect the idea, for how quickly
those things came scratching at his floor

A light appeared in the midst of all the clutter of
black,
A glimmer of grace
He removed that mask that reeked of disgust
and distaste
He lifted his head high,
And finally stood toe to toe with his enemy, face
to face.

LIFE & DEATH

Heaven is a false pretense filled with meth
Taking love from me and becoming death
How can this be purifying sins and faithfulness?

Never have had a grasp on the religion type of
thing
Always loving something that I'll lose
I wish somehow God can feel confused
Death is always a part of life
Two words that come from the dawn of time
Two in which create an awe of sublime

Swishing the verses through and through
God developed us based on two.
Created from one-and the outcome was me and
you
I can't think of a reason to which life lives
without death
In the garden, it was Eve who placed the first bet

I can't live with believing in something that will
someday disappear
Must fight these fears, holding back all my tears
Die in which, you lived your life to death
Two words becoming one, dying as two, living in
me and you

THE CAGE

The walls surround me and keep me inside,
Stopping me from ever seeing the light,
Within me is where I fear,
Within me is where I'm near
Near and dear to this cage.
Disgust fills my lungs due to the rancid smell of
this body,
Nothing can help me.
I'm stuck in this hole, tall and wide,
Humanity is distant with so much to hide.
There isn't much to do to survive,
I won't make it out alive.

I feel so electrified at the thought of fear,
Because I am aware of the reaper.
The cage I'm in isn't tattered or bruised,
But it seems that the devil is my keeper.

This cage I'm in isn't made of steel,
It isn't made of bronze, bone, or something you
can feel.
It's all in my head,
Can't remember the last time I went to bed.
Beginning to tear apart my mind,
In search of any crimes,
Maybe there's something to help mankind.

I feel so electrified at the thought of fear,
Because I am aware of the reaper.
The cage I'm in isn't tattered or bruised,
But it seems that the devil is my keeper.

Anxiety takes over some time or another,
I can't even remember my own mother.
Becoming less humane every day,
Neal down and begin to pray.
I might not live through this day,
I shall die in so much pain.
This cage is now my home,
This body will rot alone.

About the Poet

Anthony Azzarito is indeed a creative idealist and a profound poet. His lyrical/poetical content is raw, uncut, and focuses on real life problems like addiction, death, anger, self-abusiveness and other mental conflicts. He is a believer and a follower of Jesus Christ.

In his debut poetry collection, he acts as a guide for any person who deals with inner demons to know one simple thing...that they are not alone. Here you will see many rhymes and phrases welcoming you into the mind of a mad man, with the intentions of aiding all people who face adversity.

The poet was born and raised in San Diego, CA and is a US Army Veteran. He is a part of the illustrious San Diego poetry/spoken word scene and thrives on performing at local open mics and headlined at the notorious Poets Underground inside the Acid Vault.

With much love and influence from 90's and underground rap & hip hop, his performance style is very unique, and the rhyme schemes are top notch. As a refugee at a young age from drug addiction and a current fighter against anger and alcohol problems, poetry is the essential outlet. He uses the shadows of his past to bring light to others. A keen individual who certainly writes with The Ink that Bleeds...

Poets Underground Press LLC is an inclusive press that provides partnership publishing services to artists that are willing to take the challenge of becoming a professional writer. Look us up at
poetsundergroundpress.com
for more information about events, workshops and our partnership publishing program.

Poets Underground was founded in 2019 and became an official LLC in 2022. The press is run by the founder/CEO Sunny Rey Azzarito, wife of the author of this book and COO/chief-editor Anthony Azzarito. Both are published writers and host Poets Underground events throughout Southern California. They both give special thanks to their poetry community in San Diego and endless gratitude to the venue The Acid Vault who gave Poets Underground a place to call home.

Made in the USA
Monee, IL
11 October 2023